I0441895

D.I.V.A.S.

DYNAMIC

INTELLIGENT

VERSATILE

AMBITIOUS

SAVVY

BECOMING

D.I.V.A.S.

D.I.V.A.S.

SURVIVAL TIPS For a GIRL'S JOURNEY THROUGH PUBERTY

D.I.V.A.S.

DYNAMIC ~ INTELLIGENT ~ VERSATILE AMBITIOUS ~ SAVVY

HANDBOOK

By

JACQUELYN CAUTHEN R.N. B.A

Copyright © 2018 by Jacquelyn Cauthen.

Cover/Illustrations/Poetry by Jacquelyn Cauthen aka Nana Jackie
The author and publisher gratefully acknowledges Beverly Ewan, Copyeditor

ISBN: Softcover   978-1-5434-6948-6
               eBook   978-1-5434-6947-9

All rights reserved. No part of this book may be reproduced or transmitted in any form or by any means, electronic or mechanical, including photocopying, recording, or by any information storage and retrieval system, without permission in writing from the copyright owner.

Request for permission to make copies of the handbook/or copy any part of this work contact: Jacquelyn Cauthen 397 Charles Street, Bridgeport Ct., 06606

D.I.V.A.S. Workshops by appointment *e-mail: sagegardendivas@gmail.com* jackiesdivas. com Facebook Go to: Inside The Sage Garden/ Imani Heritage Mask

More Books by Jacquelyn Cauthen *MOMMAS, GRANMOMMAS AND MOTHETWIT NANA JACKIE Presents SAGE GARDEN POETRY* * *Order on-line @XLIBRIS.com, Amazon.com*

Print information available on the last page.

Rev. date: 05/01/2018

To order additional copies of this book, contact:
Xlibris
1-888-795-4274
www.Xlibris.com
Orders@Xlibris.com
770129

D.I.V.A.S. HANDBOOK
A Practical Guide for Personal Growth

Property of

Name:_____

Address:_____

City/State/Zip:_____

Date:_____

Mentor:_____

Date:_____

Club Name: _____

Club Sponsor:_____

REFLECTIONS I

Thank You for your informative information. Charmane Spence

Its very interesting Thanks Oscar Paniagua

I APPRECIATE THE TALK. HENRY TRAN.

Thank You For Stopping By One of the Best schools In the city and helping us look up to reality. Your Friend Elena Mateo

Thanks for taking the time to speak to our class MARLENE Feliz

Henry for caring. Thank for the advice. Take care of yourself Keep smiling! Tamansha

Learn alot!! Dora Sarkodie

Thank you for answering questions most of us had. Tina Padmore

I love the way you explain everything thank you. Olivia

I learned alot thank you! Lissa Luna

thankyou for the knowledge of This. Eddie Sancho

Thank you HS. Jackie for talking to us not like our mothers but like a concerned friend Phillipa

I really appreciate what you taught us Roberto PAYANO

Thank you very much for your instruction on sex and STDs. It was very helpful not only for me but for many others who need it. Esther Martinez

This is a student who really enjoyed your company. I hope you come back soon. Ebony.

50

Your session with the class was enjoyed very much by me. Thank You Stacey Herrera

THANK YOU FOR STOPING BY I ENJOYED YOUR CLASS AND PASSED INFORMATION TO OTHERS LATOYA ROBERTS.

Thank you for coming and I appreciate it very much Isha

Thank you for the lesson, I learned alot. Melissa Lorenzo

I found out the answer to many unanswered questions I had! Thanks. ANDY

Acknowledgements

Mrs. Beverly Ewan, Handbook Edit & Design
Mrs. L.Barton, Parent Coordinator PS 93X
Mrs. L. Greene, DeWitt Clinton HS Health Ed./Srs
Carol Taylor RN, Author [The Little Black Book]
Dedicated to the Village Daughters

~Past ~Present~Future~

NYC Bronx Middle & Elementary Schools:
IS 125/Henry Hudson, MS 123, IS 142, 145, 113, 129, 174,
IS 98, Hostos- Lincoln Academy, MS 391, MS 391, IS
229, MS 206B, MS 129, P.S. 93x~ 4th&5th Grd.
NYC Bronx High Schools: Evander Childs, Harry S. Truman,
Grace Dodge Vocational, Bronx Regional, Samuel Gompers,
Marble Hill International Studies, Performing Arts Academy,
Fannie Lou Hamer, Bronx Career Development, Walton,
James Monroe, James A. Rapportport, Alfred E. Smith,
DeWitt Clinton Srs.
Westchester NYS: Mt. Vernon HS, A.B. Davis MS, Mt.
Vernon, Hawthorne Pearl MS/HS,Yonkers HS / P.S.9
MLK Jr. JHS and HS/ Graham Windom Campus
NYS Teen Campers: Camp Sharparoon/Teen Valley N.Y.
Camp Minisink, N.Y./Goddard Riverside,
Rifton N.Y. Bronx Parochial Schools:
St. Anthony's, Our Lady of Grace
Connecticut
New Haven: Ladies Leadership Academy, Marrakech Inc.
Bridgeport: The Barnum School D.I.V.A.S.
Bridgeport: JACKIEs D.I.V.A.S.

For my Granddaughters

Nala Keomi, Amber Corrina,
Jasmine Brianna

TABLE OF SMARTS

HANDBOOK HIGHLIGHTS

Introduction

The Puberty Roller coaster...

I stood face to face with Lucky. Outwardly, she seemed quiet and shy, shunned by the other kids because of the braces on her teeth, shaggy unkempt hair, 1970's retro faded jeans and plaid shirt. So I agreed to be her partner. Lucky headed straight for the biggest, fastest, 'thrill of your life' Roller coaster in all of Canada— "La Ronde!"

Against my better judgment and after much begging and pleading, I agreed to go on the ride. As we strapped ourselves in, I started to get an uneasy feeling in the pit of my stomach. With mounting trepidation I watched Lucky, with eyes closed and head bowed, clutching the crucifix around her neck as she made the sign of the cross then kissed it and settled back into her seat. As two attendants checked that we were secure in our seats, I said my own prayers and thought to myself, "BIG MISTAKE!" Seconds later, my stomach fell to the floor of the cab. Fear propelled my heart faster than the normal 70 -80 beats per minute. I heard voices screaming and realized mine was one of them. I wanted to kill Lucky, but I was paralyzed: my arms and legs plastered to the torpedo-like capsule, jerking and swaying every which way. I felt a crushing force like a bowling ball attached to my neck.

With my eyes tightly closed I could see the local newspaper headline, "**Camp Nurse Has Heart Attack and Dies on Roller Coaster at local Amusement Park**." Not knowing when sanity would return to me, I prayed for forgiveness for anything I had ever done to anyone at any time, while silently pleading, DEAR GOD WHY ME??? Just when I thought the ride was over, I opened my eyes to discover we were at the highest point of the ride— I thought to myself 'will this ever end??' The ride began again, over the same tracks only backwards. It was the longest ninety seconds of my life. Once I was standing on solid ground, I vowed to never, ever get on a roller coaster again— NEVER!

Yet, I knew I couldn't really be mad at Lucky. I chose, against my better judgment to go on the ride with her and I was *still alive.* Did I ever get on a roller coaster again? Yes, years later, with my five-year-old grandson at Six Flags Amusement park. He was not afraid and invited me to join him on the 'kiddy' ride. Release my fears I faced the challenge once more, I knew I would live through it— and I did!

Is Puberty life's Roller coaster?

Here's what I know. You can't choose where, when, or how hormones (chemical messengers) begin their work. In young women this messenger hormone is called *Estrogen.* Puberty is that part of Teen life, also called adolescence, which signals your beginning journey toward Womanhood. Separating fact from fiction is necessary to understanding the 'roller coaster' effect of puberty and sexual development. Also, there is the challenge of finding a balance in how you respond to the ups and downs, the sideways and inside-out emotions that can leave preteens and teens suffering from feelings of roller coaster 'whiplash', at any given moment! Just remember— help is always near. There are valuable lessons to be learned while on the roller coaster, and like many young women before you, me included, you will survive!

PUBERTY IS
A Poem for My Daughters

Puberty is a Feeling
that you feel /when you feel
that you feel /it's a feeling
that you never felt before
Or
Puberty is a Sensation
that you sense /when you sense
that you sense/ it's a sensation
that you never sensed before
Or
Puberty is a Thought
that you think /when you think
that you think /it's a thought
that you never
thunk before
Or
in Mother words
Puberty is...
Feelings,
Sensations and Thoughts
That lets you know
It's time for
the Daughters to Grow—
UP Got it!!!

BECOMING D.I.V.A.S.

D.I.V.A.S. is the acronym for Dynamic, Intelligent, Versatile, Ambitious, and Savvy; and represents *affirmative values* to enhance a girl's experience as she grows and matures. My main goal in designing the Handbook and program is for you to BECOME— ALERT, INFORMED, EDUCATED, PREPARED and RESPONSIBLE, in thought, word, and deed. This is how you affirm the D.I.V.A.S. values. It is important that you understand that the beginning and on-going changes that happen to your body are all part of adolescent female growth and development. These normal body changes, commonly known as puberty, happen to girls everywhere. These changes give rise to all kinds of questions, dilemmas, 'crisis' and uneasiness. The *SMARTS* are listed in simple and easy to understand answers, activities, and tips. By following these 'survival tips' you are certain to develop a positive mindset and positive habits: all of which will support you on your journey as you "grow up" and mature. Also, as you mature, the sexual attitudes and behaviors that leads to your attraction to the opposite sex, are all normal. So naturally, sooner or later, having a boyfriend or dating will become a major issue. Just remember— you always have CHOICES.

It's Time for Answers ...

For those girls who are wondering: Who am I Now? Am I pretty enough to enter a Beauty Pageant? Will I grow-up to be famous? Can I become a Singer or Rapper or Musician? Questions and more questions! During puberty every girl grows and develops at her own pace. To help build your self-esteem apply all the SMARTS, Activities and Alerts in the hand book at your own pace. Unfortunately, in today's society, nearly nine out of ten girls stop doing what they love because of fretfulness about their looks. Too often, for some, the word 'Diva' is limited to describe physical looks, highlight sex appeal, or to describe as participants in over the top non-sense and offer sensational (silly) TV shows. Behaviors and attitudes here are sometimes negative, DISRESPECTFUL, and immature. Regrettably, certain female entertainers use the word to describe themselves with this limited definition. While this is true, the word Diva can also be translated as 'a powerful feminine presence' or *Goddess-a woman of great Beauty or Grace.'*

You are very special... In all the world there is no one like you. No one knows your 'feelings, sensations, or thoughts'. *You are unique because only you look like you. And, guess what—*anyone can be made to look beautiful on the outside and still be ugly on the inside. Sadly, when someone is not feeling good about their self they may show signs of ugliness in their behavior and attitude. Some examples of inside ugliness include anger, envy, sadness, greed, selfishness, bullying, gossiping, name-calling and intolerance. "Beauty is only skin deep" is a message my Mother gave me. She taught to me to believe that I was beautiful and that my outside beauty must be balanced by my inside beauty. My Mother was rich in knowledge and wisdom, and always told me I was very special. Believing this, I utilized the knowledge, values, and morals she instilled in me. Like you, I experienced all the normal teen changes and challenges every girl faces during puberty. I remember having several neighborhood mamas many good friends and Club members. Become active and find a mentor (for yourself) or sponsor (for you club) from your family, your Church, Community, or School (teachers and counselors). Choose an adult you know and ask them to assist your participation in the D.I.V.A.S. Handbook and Participant Completion Activities.

I AM
DYNAMIC

EVERY DAY I AM VIBRANT, STRONGER, AND HAVE MORE ENERGY

BODY AND EXERCISE SMART

#1
SHAPE UP: The **number #1** fitness exercise is walking.

#2
Walk 15 minutes away from home and walk 15 minutes back home 3X to 5X a week. Make it a habit.

#3
Get a *buddy or partners* to keep you company and keep you motivated.

#4
You can also jog, run, jump rope, dance, roller skate, ice skate, hike, and bike: Make exercise FUN!

#5
The best water exercise is swimming. You must learn to swim, the sooner the better.

#6
Join a school/community team and participate in any regular group athletic activity 3-5X a week. Try something new!

#7
Do not exercise through the pain. Pain is a signal to STOP.'No pain, no gain" is an exercise myth. It is possible that you may have soreness when you initially start to exercise.

ACTIVITY: Start a Dance or Exercise Club. List 10 exercises or athletic activities you think you would like to do. Share this with 5 to 10 good friends. Choose one or more activities. YES YOU CAN!

HYGIENE SMART

Personal hygiene is the practice of good health habits. This means that cleansing and caring for <u>yourself</u> becomes part of your daily routine.

8
Take a shower or bath every day, your body scent is stronger. Also have your own personal soap. Soap is not an option: it is a MUST!

9
Use deodorants, after shower or bath and have your own skin care products.

10
Do not spray or put roll-on deodorant on top of sweat or funk, this really makes a bad 'funky' odor worse.

11
Stay away from deodorants that are heavily perfumed, scented, or labeled anti-perspirant.

ALERT: Sweating is normal. **Be aware:** many anti-perspirants have irritating or toxic chemicals that can clog your pores and sweat glands, so that the pores do not work properly. Also, these products usually cost more money.

MENSES OR 'PERIOD' SMART

The menstrual cycle is more commonly called the Menses or Period. All females have special 'egg' cells that begin to grow and mature, once a month, usually one at a time. Once you have started your menses or your period you have to pay very close attention to your body's menstrual cycle. You will know when this begins because you will have a menstrual flow (bloody stream). At this point your body is maturing so that you can now become a Mother.

12
NOW is the time to select a women's health provider, who is also known as a Gynecologist. You can choose a female health professional [APRN] or female MD. It's your choice!

13
Use a personal calendar to chart and record your "period" dates, the number of days, and the type of flow (light, medium, heavy).

14
Throughout the beginning (1st to 3rd) years of your menstrual cycle, make this charting routine a monthly habit. It is important that this becomes your responsibility.

15
The body scent (odor) becomes much stronger as sweat glands become more active, this is to be expected.

ALERT: Beware of myths and untruths. Fact—it is safe to wash your hair, take a bath or go swimming. Most of the time, you can do any and all activities and being active help your 'feeling good'.

16
When thirsty— drink water! This will help all the body systems eliminate waste and decrease your body odor.

17
Do not pick/pop/squeeze pimples or whiteheads, this could lead to an inflammation and infection. Learn what is safe to do, what soaps, lotions, or products to use, depending on your skin type.

18
If this becomes a serious facial 'skin problem' concern, also called Acne, seek a Dermatologist or Adolescent (Teen) Health and medical provider.

19
Do total body skin care daily, when showering or bathing, using two washcloths. Use one wash cloth for your face, and the second wash cloth for the body and private areas.

20
Learn to wash your hair daily or weekly or as regularly **as needed.** This hair care will be based on your hair's body and texture.

21
It's a really good idea to talk to a mature adult, and read a teen health *book about the details of puberty changes.
*see D.I.V.A.S. Book list [#5]

22
Keep track of your own supply of feminine hygiene products such as sanitary pads, panty-liners, pads or tampons. In time you will determine which product is best for your life style.

23
Be prepared and carry an extra sanitary pad or panty liner for any emergencies.

24
Change all undergarments: bras, panties, tee shirts, tights and spandex pants daily. **Wash your personal underwear.** Not doing this invites dust mites and other germs to live in dirty "funky" clothing, causing itching, allergy, infection or disease.

25
Keep your personal feminine hygiene and grooming items in a special Toiletry Bag or Pouch.

26
Being mature means being responsible. You should always have an extra bar of soap and deodorant.

ACTIVITY: Go to a Drug Store (pharmacy) and explore the feminine hygiene section. Before using any feminine products, external or internal, carefully **read** all directions for product use and product disposal, this too is your responsibility. Remember to discuss this with your Mom/Mentor.

I AM
INTELLIGENT

I AM AN INTELLECTUAL

MINDSET SMART

Puberty hormones affect your feelings, sensations, and your mindset or your thoughts. Sometimes you feel up, sometimes you feel down, sometimes you feel upside down—and you don't Why. This happens to many girls and it's normal. Below are the smarts you can practice to help develop and maintain a positive and healthy mindset. Things will balance out as you mature.

27
Do not spend daylight hours just watching TV, playing online video games (internet) or on the phone texting/twitter/talking/tweeting. ***Anything*** *you do/say/show on the internet-stays there FOREVER!!!*

28
Give yourself a time out, a 10-15 minute rest period, when needed. It's okay to take a nap (30 to 60 minutes).

29
Eliminate all electronic and computer activities at least **2** hours before bedtime. To fully REST the brain and body: make it a nightly habit to get 8—9 hours of sleep.

30
It is important that you STOP all activity. Stop means turning off the; T.V., Radio, IPOD, Smart phone, Video games, computer, ear phones too. These are all unhealthy distractions. It gets even worse.

ALERT: When you are asleep your body's systems are fully restored and prepare you for the next day. Not getting enough sleep is like being in a car that runs out of gas. Everything stops!

KNOWLEDGE AND WORD SMART

 # 31
Join with people who like gathering together, sharing ideas and using their words. Join or start a Poetry, Spoken Word, or Debate Club.

 # 32
Learn to read, write and speak English correctly

 # 33
Learn the art of public speaking.

 # 34
Whenever possible learn a second (another) language. In today's world, being Bi- lingual is an definite advantage

 # 35
Increase your vocabulary or word power by learning and using at least 10 to 20 new words every week: <u>on your own</u>. Start by identifying new words right here in the handbook. JUST DO IT!

ACTIVITY: Read "*NANA JACKIE presents SAGE GARDEN POETRY*: A Literacy through Poetry Workbook

ALERT: You are not a nerd because you use your words wisely and choose to speak with intelligence. You are an intellectual because you chose to increase your vocabulary and use correct grammar!

LITERARY AND BOOK SMART

Start a D.I.V.A.S. <u>Book</u> of the month <u>Club</u> with three or more people like you, who enjoy reading. As the group grows, each person contributes the book they have chosen, for the month. Getting started:

1. *Choose a new book every month*
2. *Have theme book club reviews: dress-up/act out*
3. *Pick the same day/date & location to discuss Book*

<u>Booklist:</u>

1. Stay Strong: Simple Life Lessons~ By *Terrie Williams**
2. Of Thee I Sing-A Letter to My Daughters ~ By *Barack H. Obama*
3. Yes I Can~ By *Devon Harris* *
4. Can I Have Some Money? ~ By *Candi Sparks**
5. Changing Bodies, Changing Lives~ By *Ruth Bell*
6. Grandma Buddy's House ~ By *Betty Stallings- Murray**
7. Puzzles Are Us ~ By Kevin Ikim Dunn *
8. My Sister, My Friend ~ By Barbara Dominick*
9. Blue Moon ~ By Alicia Keyes
10. Who Moved My Cheese? For Teens ~ By *Spencer Johnson*

*** Authors I Have Known

STREET SMART

 # 36
Let an adult know where you are at all times.

 # 37
Protect yourself: 1-Avoid deserted streets or deserted buildings.
2-Pay attention when traveling alone: STAY WOKE!!!

 # 38
Be aware when you enter or leave your house/apartment. **STOP!**
Look around first. See if anyone is standing nearby. If you do not
know them, wait for them to move away or watch them carefully
as you quickly move past them.

 # 39
If you are home alone **never** opens the door for strangers even if
they call or know your name.

 # 40
Do not ride in elevators alone or with strangers.

 # 41
Play it smart when riding on subway trains. Ride near the conductor
whenever possible.

ACTIVITY: Street smart survival means identifying positive and
negative feelings and behaviors, in others and yourself. Read the
parable *"Two Wolves"* with your mentor and discuss what this means
this means to you. ** Find *Two Wolves* on the internet.

STREET SMART

42
Use "safe" waiting areas near other people. You do not need to check or look or see if the train is coming.

43
When traveling on buses— always ride close to the front or near

44
You must use the car seat belt. In most places, it's the law.

45
Do not accept lifts (rides) or gifts from strangers, under any circumstance.

46
When traveling or while in transit— if a group of your friends or other strangers are misbehaving **move** to a safer more quiet area

ALERT: Texting, Tweeting, and using IPods or cell phones while walking is hazardous to your personal safety. The second most stolen electronic device is your smart/cell phone and your life could be at stake— STAY WOKE!

STREET SMART

47
Do not accept or tolerate verbal or physical bullying for any reason, under any circumstance.

48
If you are being bullied or know someone who is you must tell somebody **immediately;** like a parent, guardian, counselor or mature adult.

49
Beware of cyberspace and internet bullies. Bullying here can really become as big a problem as face-to-face conflict. Once again, you must tell a parent, guardian, counselor or mature adult.

50
Join a school/church/community anti-bulling club. Here, you can get support or give support to friends and peers.

ACTIVITY: If you cannot find or do not have a school, community, or local group support, there are people who can support you. Visit the web site www.stopbullying.com

MY PLEDGE OF NON-VIOLENCE

I promise that
I will do my best to
refrain from participating
in acts of violence or bullying
in my home, in my school
and in my neighborhood.

I also promise to stand
with the sisterhood and
other human beings
who are treated unfairly.

By doing this
I make known
how very special I am.

I will remember that I
want to live in a peaceful world,
and by taking this pledge
I will be doing my part
to achieve this goal.

[AUTHOR UNKNOWN]

I AM
VERSATILE

I AM HEALTHY OF
MIND, BODY AND SPIRIT

A ROOM FULL OF D.I.V.A.S.

'NAMASTE' said the Sage to
A Room Full of D.I.V.A.S.
She expected their best
manners and decorum
none failed the test
all gave respect
the Hip- Hoppers
the Cheerleaders/Athletes
Scholars and Mathematicians
Step–teams/track teams
Class Leaders/each one
Able/Capable and DYNAMIC

They filled the room
like Butterflies
Babywomen Flutterbyes
some had the
talkative gene
they wanted to be heard and seen
the TAH-DAH twins
Amber C. Loquacious
and Nala K. Courageous
made everyone personalized
Affirmation mugs
inscribed with gold letters
"I am an INTELLECTUAL"

Poets, Writers, Artist
created the mural
on the meeting room wall
"Gabby" Douglas ~ Mo'ne Davis
Alia Atkinson ~Malala Yousafzai
Honored for doing/for being
audacious and AMBITIOUS
the message here
so very clear
'You are talented and gifted
dream big dreams
Creativity and VERSATILITY
Have no boundary

Rosebuds of Promise sang
as Praise Dancers danced
to I need' "A Little More Jesus'
Faith, Hope, Charity and
the Rainbow Sisters
made tee-shirts that read
I AM SAVVY
GOT KNOW-HOW!
in celebration of their
Individuality and Camaraderie
leaving with Peace and Harmony
'NAMASTE' said the Sage to
A Room Full of D.I.V.A.S.

VERSATILE AND MULTI-TALENTED SMART

Versatility or Skillfulness occurs when you are willing to experience and creatively participate in any area or endeavor you put your mind to. I believe that we are all versatile and can become outstanding as Writers, Scholars, Scientists, Musicians, Artists, Poets, and so on— when YOU choose to. Many multi-talented folk realize that versatility also encourages resourcefulness, flexibility and most of all fosters originality.

51
MUSIC: Take singing, dancing or instrument lessons. Try something new and different from what you already know.

52
ART: Take art classes or workshops. Study different methods, various tools and materials used in artwork. Experience the fun of making "something out of nothing".

53
RECREATION: Plan regular indoor game nights or game days (outdoors).Play board games and card games, *face to face.* Girls can safely play in team or individual sports. *Competition* teaches you how to win and lose

54
PERFORMANCE: Join a **Drama club,** where you can learn theatrical and stage skills, including public speaking.

55
ACADEMICS /HISTORIANS- Enter Writing, Debating and Mind Building/scholarly contest. Participate in Science Fairs, Spelling Bees, Chess Tournaments, Board games and more. Doing your best always makes you a winner!

NUTRITIOUS SMART

 # 56
Pay attention to what you put into your body. Food choices greatly affect your 'Mind, Body, and Spirit': YOU ARE WHAT YOU EAT and DRINK!

 # 57
Start every day with Breakfast and drink 100% natural _fruit juices_ rather than fruit drinks Remember, most fruit juices need to be refrigerated. Breakfast should be made a morning habit.

 # 58
Decrease or eliminate all soda and artificially colored and chemically flavored sugary _fruit drinks_. When you are thirsty it is a signal that your body needs more hydration.

 # 59
Drink water first! Goal #1 = Drink 6-8 glasses of liquid a day (in a 24 hour period). Water will help all the body systems cleanse and work properly while allowing your body to release toxins and waste.

 # 60
Learn the importance of eating wholesome foods and make it a daily habit of eating four to five or more servings of fruits and vegetables. Dried fruits and nuts are also good snacks.

 # 61
Learn everything you can about 'living foods', wheatgrass, wheatgrass juice and probiotics

ACTIVITY: Visit and explore a Natural or Holistic health food store, find out about nature's Herbs and Spices and try different Teas.

62

Limit your intake of fast foods and processed or modified foods. These foods have little nutrition value and most of them are filled with extra salt and other chemicals that are harmful to you.

63

Every mealtime plate should have vegetables, salads or fruits [every color of the rainbow] Experiment with different seasonings.

64

Eat as little animal fat or fatty foods or oils as possible. Olive oil, Coconut oil, and Grape seed oil, are much healthier and are great substitutes.

65

Decrease or eliminate drinking regular COW'S (whole) MILK. It is not a beverage; it is a food that often causes stomach cramping, gas pains, and discomfort. This is a problem for many people and is also known as lactose or milk sugar intolerance.

66

Most cakes and cookies, and things like chips, nips, all candies are great tasty treats but are full of processed/artificial sugar.

67

Start eliminating white or cane sugar whenever possible. Try natural sweeteners, like Honey, Agave or use fruits.

ALERT: White sugar or cane sugar is extremely addictive: this means the more of it you eat, the more you want. Too much sugar can lead to hyperactivity or more serious health issues.

I AM
AMBITIOUS

I AM FREE TO BE AND ACHIEVE WHATEVER I CHOOSE

INSIDE THE SAGE GARDEN

Inside the Sage Garden
you can journey to that
special mind-place to
feel what you write
express yourself
write what you feel
It's your own space
Here words can be magical
words can be fun
Use your imagination
make up one—it's Soulacious
tell your story/think prose
describe/record/reward
your life/compose
write away stress
Be courageous
Release all fears/be bold
Be outrageous
put pen to scroll
there is no wrong
there is no right
only writer's delight
Whatever you do —it's personal
the journaling is up to you
Inside the Sage Garden

JOURNAL SMART

'Inside The Sage Garden'_is the name I have given to the mind 'space' where your words can become part of a wonderful never ending story. Here creativity and imagination is available for everyone. I invite you join me and start your own journal. For now, don't worry about writing skills. The more you write, the better your handwriting, spelling, grammar, vocabulary, and future writing skills will become.

Keeping a journal is a wonderful way to tell your story or tell a story, using real life live events [facts]. Or you can make up a story, where you determine the subject matter [fictions]. I began keeping a Dairy and my stories as a pre-teen. Start your journal TODAY!

68
It is important to date each journal entry using: month/day/year.

69
Select a location and time where you have privacy and quiet.

70
Experiment with different writing styles. There is no wrong way to write your journal or wrong subject matter to enter.

I ENJOY WRITING AND I WRITE EVERY DAY

WELL-BEING SMART

71
Well-being happens when your inside beauty embraces and is equal to your outside beauty

AFFIRMATIONS: A positive statements, or promise and declaration of a truth and reflects your inside beauty. Make large signs with one affirmation printed on each sign and post signs where you can see them [on walls /doors/mirrors] and speak them aloud.

I~   EVERYDAY I AM VIBRANT STRONGER AND I HAVE MORE ENERGY

II~   I AM GIFTED AND TALENTED

III~   I AM AN INTELLECTUAL

IV~   I AM LOVABLE AND CAPABLE

V~   I AM HEALTHY OF MIND, BODY AND SPIRIT

VI~   I AM NATURALLY BEAUTIFUL

VII~   I AM FREE TO BE AND ACHIEVE WHATEVER I CHOOSE

VIII~   I ENJOY WRITING AND I WRITE EVERYDAY

IX~   I AM THANKFUL FOR INCREASING CONFIDENCE AND GIRL POWER

X~   I AM BLESSED AND HIGHLY FAVORED

HEALTH CARE SMART

It's smart to be educated and active in your health care. It's your body and it's important to 1) learn the name and location of reproductive (puberty) body parts 2) understand how they work as your body grows and develops 3) know how to care for and keep yourself in the best of health.

#72
You must have an Annual Physical Exam. The medical provider or doctor will get your medical history and check your body for normal healthy growth and development.

#73
Once you have started to experience your menses a regular basis you will need to see a Gynecologist or Adolescent provider who specializes in Women's Health.

#74
Place the provider information below in a place that's easy to remember/locate. **Then Memorize it.

#75
Gynecologist/Provider Information (Print):
MD/PNP/P.A.:_____
Hospital/Clinic:_____
Telephone: _____
Your Blood Type _____**Allergies_____

75 (Cont'd)
**EMERGENCY CONTACTS (Print):

#1) NAME_____

ADDRESS:_____

**PHONE:_____

CITY:_____STATE_____ZIP_____

**#2) NAME:_____

ADDRESS:_____

**PHONE:_____

CITY:_____STATE_____ZIP_____

76
FIRST AID Rule # 1: DON'T PANIC. Know what to do, know where to go, and who to call in an EMERGENCY. Memorize the phone numbers of two responsible adults

77
For emergency Call 911, STAY CALM and talk clearly – **do not** hang up until help arrives.

ACTIVITY: In many local areas and school districts the American Red Cross [ARC] offers free school based First Aid, Health and Safety courses. If this is not readily available Call your local ARC Chapter. Do Sign up and take a Basic First Aid course. ARC also enlist Teens over 14 to volunteer for community service.

MONEY AND MATH SMART

 # 78
Be prepared to earn an allowance by doing household chores, or find and sell a product or service others may need. For example: offer to assist someone elderly or infirm/on a regular basis.

 # 79
Learn how to budget money earned or money gifts [save some] A budget is a written plan of action for spending money.

 # 80
If you get an allowance or earn money on a regular basis [weekly or monthly] basis, be sure to save some!

 # 81
Do not carry large sums of money; do not carry it all in one place, and DO NOT DISPLAY OR ANNOUNCE YOUR MONEY.

 # 82
Learn basic Arithmetic, **memorize** the number rules and the times table from 1-12— they never change!! This will make your learning higher Math skills much easier.

ACTIVITY: Investigate what teen entrepreneurs are doing, budgeting, and money management. [Read book #4]

ALERT: Girls are as equally good at mathematics and numbers as boys. Many become business executives, professionals, financial coaches. Knowing basic math and money management are necessary skills. More often than not, women are in charge of their household budgets.

D.I.V.A.S.~<u>YOU ARE VERY SPECIAL</u>
Vision Board

Write 5 things/ways that make you very special

1._____
_____
2._____
_____
3._____
_____
4._____
_____
5._____
_____

Write 5 ideas that you would like to do in the future

6._____
_____
7._____
_____
8._____
_____
9._____
_____
10._____
_____

Activity: Make a collage. Draw, paint, cut and paste pictures and words that represent you. #1-5=Who are you now? #6-10 =Who do want to be? Have FUN!

I AM SAVVY

I AM THANKFUL FOR INCREASING CONFIDENCE AND GIRL POWER

"RUN AWAY FROM TOXIC PEOPLE."
Instead, surround yourself
with others who are positive,
who support you
and want you to succeed."

—Tererai Trent, PhD
Zimbabwean Educator

DRUG-USE SMART

Consuming illegal (street) drugs will lead to changes in your behavior. These changes go from hard to control or high energy to low or no energy. Consuming these could cause serious harm to your mind and body.

83
Drink as little coffee as possible, it has a chemical in it called caffeine that may cause you to become *'hyper'* or overly excited.

84
Do not accept or drink alcoholic beverages like beer, wine coolers, or wine without parental permission. If you are under 21 consumption by you is illegal (in most places

85
Do not smoke or put tobacco products in your body.

86
Do not smoke weed or marijuana. This drug decreases your ability to focus and is unsafe for your thinking and your ability to make healthy decisions.

87
Do not use illegal drugs or 'pop' pills—Over use or increase prescription medications-- these could harm your brain.

ALERT: If you need to take prescription or over-the-counter medications (drugs) you should know as much about the drug as possible. This means understanding the good, side and bad or toxic (poisonous) effects. Most of these drugs are considered legal and Pharmacies will print out this information for you: READ IT.

DATE SMART

88
When thinking about having a boyfriend or partner, begin by looking for a good or positive person and <u>establish a friendship</u> first. What things do you have in common? Think about it.

89
Do not set up 'home alone' dates. Respect yourself. Demand respect for yourself from others.

90
Do not go out with anyone whom your parents or guardians have not met and know nothing about.

91
Do not accept unseen 'BLIND' dates from internet chat rooms, face book, you tube, twitter, or unknown 'cyberspace' persons.

92
Do not send or share or receive personal information or **photos** with strangers or casual acquaintances on the internet. Once this information is on the internet it cannot be erased (it lives there forever). It can be 'grabbed' or stolen by anyone at any time.

ALERT: Do not lower your standards to please anybody—neither friend(s) nor acquaintance(s). No matter how friendly he appears to be. There should be absolutely No communication with adult strangers. [Strangers are people you have not/cannot bring home]

BEAUTY SMART

93
You really don't need to wear any make-up on a regular basis unless you are a model or performer. Of course there are exceptions for special events.

94
Clear lip gloss is okay if you need to moisten your lips. A light Lipstick can be worn on special occasions or for special occasions.

95
Eye liner and eye shadow is for more mature women, who may wear make-up as part of their daily routine.

96
Do not use make-up to look older and NEVER lie about your age. Deception here will only lead to unwanted attention from older boys or men.

97
You do not need to wear makeup, you're *okay*. Being confident, capable, and feeling good about your natural or physical (outside beauty) appearance is more important than 'cosmetics'.

I AM NATURALLY
BEAUTIFUL

SEXUALITY SMART

Often the growth of the girl's reproductive organs and the release of puberty hormones make you feel, sense, and think differently—especially when it comes to boys. Sexual interest, consciousness, and exploration are heightened. This is normal. It is very important that you discuss and understand how to protect your "sexuality" or "your sexy" with your mentor and <u>adult you trust.</u>

GROW YOUR SEXUALITY VOCABULARY

Abstinence: the practice of not being physically involved or having sexual (bodily) contact with the opposite sex.

Virgin: the title given to a woman who does not have sexual relationships or partners. This is also called abstinence.

Hormone: a chemical messenger that travels from one part of the body to another part of the body, giving instructions for growth, development, and body functions.

Estrogen: a hormone produced by a woman's body that makes her develop typical female sexual features and prepares her body for having a baby.

Pedophiles: the name given to BAD adults who like to touch, play with, misuse and abuse children by touching their body.

Molestation: the word describing anyone that forces undesired sexual attention and behaviors (touches peoples private parts) without their permission.

<u>YOU HAVE THE RIGHT TO SAY NO</u>

"NO doesn't mean never

It means waiting

For the right person

For the right place

For the right time

For the right circumstances"

[AUTHOR UNKNOWN]

SEXUALITY SMART CONT'D

 # 98
NO means NO. Remember--**No one** should touch, grab, pinch, or 'playfully' squeeze your body anywhere—against your will.

 # 99
If any person has approached you or touched your body against your will— TELL an adult or authority person immediately.

 # 100
Anyone who really cares for you or says "I love you' will not force you to do anything you don't want to do. Nor should they physically hit, beat, verbally or emotionally abuse and hurt you.

ACTIVITY: Join a Community or Health-based Teen Program where you can talk about your feelings, relationships and emotions, on a regular basis. Here, you will find youth counselors, adults and other mentors you can TRUST, talk to and confide in. These adults sincerely care about your well-being and will give you guidance and Protect you!

I AM
LOVABLE AND CAPABLE

DAILY PLEDGE

I AM A VOICE AND I AM A LEADER
I WILL LEAD AND NOT FOLLOW
I WILL BELIEVE NOT DOUBT
I WILL CREATE NOT DESTROY
I AM A FORCE FOR GOOD
I WILL DEFY THE ODDS
I WILL SET A NEW STANDARD
STEP UP, STEP UP, STEP UP!

[Author unknown]

~ Message To The Village Daughters ~

Aspire to achieve your goals...

For as long as I can remember— I had a burning desire to become a nurse. I declared this vocation at the age of five. I wanted to be the first in my family to become a professional. After high school, I went to the Mount Sinai Hospital School of Nursing School with a full scholarship, and the support of my family. By the age of twenty, I had achieved my first major goal. I was a Professional Registered Nurse, specializing in Pediatrics and Adolescent Health care. Over a period of twenty years, I continued my journey as a Teen Health Educator and Life Skills/Success Coach, _facilitating_ and presenting Health Education seminars to thousands of N.YC public and parochial school students

Many of the Handbook 100+ Smarts, Alerts and Activities are based on "the facts" and my personal and professional relationships with Preteen and Teen girls. Whether you have a burning desire or passion, or you have dreams or goals, the more you know about YOU, the better you feel about you—the closer you get to achieving all your goals.

I expect you to succeed...

It was during my teen years that I realized what my grandmother meant when she said *"don't nothing beat a failure but a try"*. At first, I thought it was a riddle. As I matured I came to understand that if you try something, if you meet the challenge, if you do your best—but don't succeed— you are not a failure. Failure is an event. Do not let any event or any person label you a failure. Do not let anyone 'label' you period. Remember, You are a person— not an event. These things I sincerely believe. *You are very **Special**—You are **Unique**—You have **Value.***

Lastly, I am confident that this Handbook will arm every girl with the tools needed to "survive" this journey called Puberty. My best hope is that the information within will allow you to feel good about you and lead you to form positive relationships with girls like you. Tell a good friend. I invite you to join the D.I.V.A.S. Sisterhood, build a network of peer support and look for positive mentors 'mamas' from your community, our Village. I am just one of them.

NAMASTE
NANA JACKIE

D.I.V.A.S. Completion Activities

1. Re-read Hand Book: underline and highlight words and passages as need be—it's *your handbook!*
2. *Chose* an adult mentor to review and discuss handbook with you, assist with on line/off line registration and web site. The mentor will also sign your certificate.
3. Get a calendar and mark the date(s) to complete each and any all activities recommended throughout the Handbook. This may take some awhile—commit your time.
4. Membership Registration Options: Sign and Laminate your membership card locally Club Membership List: You can register yourself and/or your D.I.V.A.S Club (Exercise/Drama/Dance/ Poetry/ Social/ Entrepreneurship club etc.) by email** or mail to info:

   > Att: JACKIE'S DIVAS Jacquelyn Cauthen, 397 Charles St. Bridgeport,Ct. 06606 Seminars and Workshops by appointment contact: Nana Jackie at sagegardendivas@gmail.com
   > www.jackiesdivas.com

5. Post your D.I.V.A.S. Certification of Completion
6. Clubs with 12 Registered Members can receive Club membership Certificate, Register Club on Website, and also receive a Certificate(s) of Participation for each Member.

D.I.V.A.S. Club: Basic Set-Up

1. Clubs should meet on a regular basis
2. Weekly, Bi-monthly, or Monthly
3. Choose a safe and easy to reach location
4. Use sample registration form/Pg. 42 (or design your own)
5. Enlist Mentor participation or guidance

SOCIAL Club— Establish a hobby or activity that always makes you feel good and invite 2-10 girls to join you. Attend positive and cultural activities in your community and beyond

SCIENCE & MATH Club - Join other girl 'Techies' * for some ideas READ or View 'Hidden Figures "and go to www.techbridge.com

ENTREPRENEURSHIP & ART Club – Establish a hobby or activity that you can sell as a product or service for profit.

1. Visit IMANI HERITAGE MASK page on Facebook. Entrepreneurs can see NANA JACKIE *Artist
2. Visit Xlibris.com to review 'Nana Jackie presents Sage Garden Poetry".

Write YOUR CLUB Ideas:

_____

_____

_____

_____

_____

_____

Club Name_____

Location/Address_____

City/State_____

D.I.V.A.S. Club Membership List:

1._____

2._____

3._____

4._____

5._____

6._____

7._____

8._____

9._____

10._____

11._____

12._____

Reminder: Use the Daily Pledge to start your D.I.V.A.S. Club meetings. Be sure to register your club on line or via mail and *network* with other D.I.V.A.S.

Go to: www.jackiesdivas.com

BECOMING D.I.V.A.S. Contact/Order form

Name_____

Address_____

City/State/Zip_____

Phone(h)_____(c)_____

Email_____

I would like to Order:	#Copies	$Cost	Total
D.I.V.A.S. Handbook	_____	X $ 10.00	_____
D.I.V.A.S. Journal	_____	X $ 7.00	_____
Sage Garden Poetry	_____	X $15.00	_____
Sage Garden DVD	_____	X $ 7.00	_____

Add Sales Tax [% residents state tax] $ _____   _____

Add Shipping $2.95 [1 books/1 DVD] $ _____   _____

Totals : $ _____   _____

Pay by Check or Money order or Pay Pal --
Mail to: Jacquelyn Cauthen, 397 Charles St. Bridgeport, CT 06606

Support for D.I.V.A.S. Teens & Mentors:
I would like Information about Workshops

_____ **Leadership Skills**   _____**Time Managemen**

_____ **Fitness and Nutrition**   _____ **Holistic Health**

_____ **Wealth Building**   _____ **Public Speaking**

_____ **12 Universal Laws Success/ Teen Life Skills**

_____ **Personal Health Safety and Healthy Environment**

_____ **Life Skills & Resource Management [co-ed]**

_____ **Literacy Through Poetry [co-ed]**

Aspire to achieve your goals...

I expect you to succeed...

Thank you Jackie! I found your lesson to be very informative and useful.
— Jessica Maikena

Thank you very much for the information. I found it to be very useful and insightful. I'd be very happy to pass the info along. Thank you again!! — Jennifer Rios

Ms. Jackie
thank you for the lesson. It was very interesting and informative.
— Damion Marshall

Thanks for informing us. and educating us.
— Soren —

Thank u so much. Now I believe in abstinance!
— Anthony

I could talk to my girl about it and pass I information
— Terry Vea

You openness and honesty was refreshing &

Thank you very relaxing to the enviornment

Thank you for sharing your thoughts with us. am really grateful.
— Sandra

during your presentation which was very informative.

Good Job

Thank you

Thanks for the info hope you come back
Hello! Lynx

Ms. JACKIE, THANK YOU!! YOUR LESSON WAS VERY INFORMATIVE.
— JONATHAN.

Ms. Jackie thank you for being very blunt and informative.

Ms. Jackie, thank you for been here with us and spend you time teaching us about that important subject.
— Imallely.

REFLECTIONS III

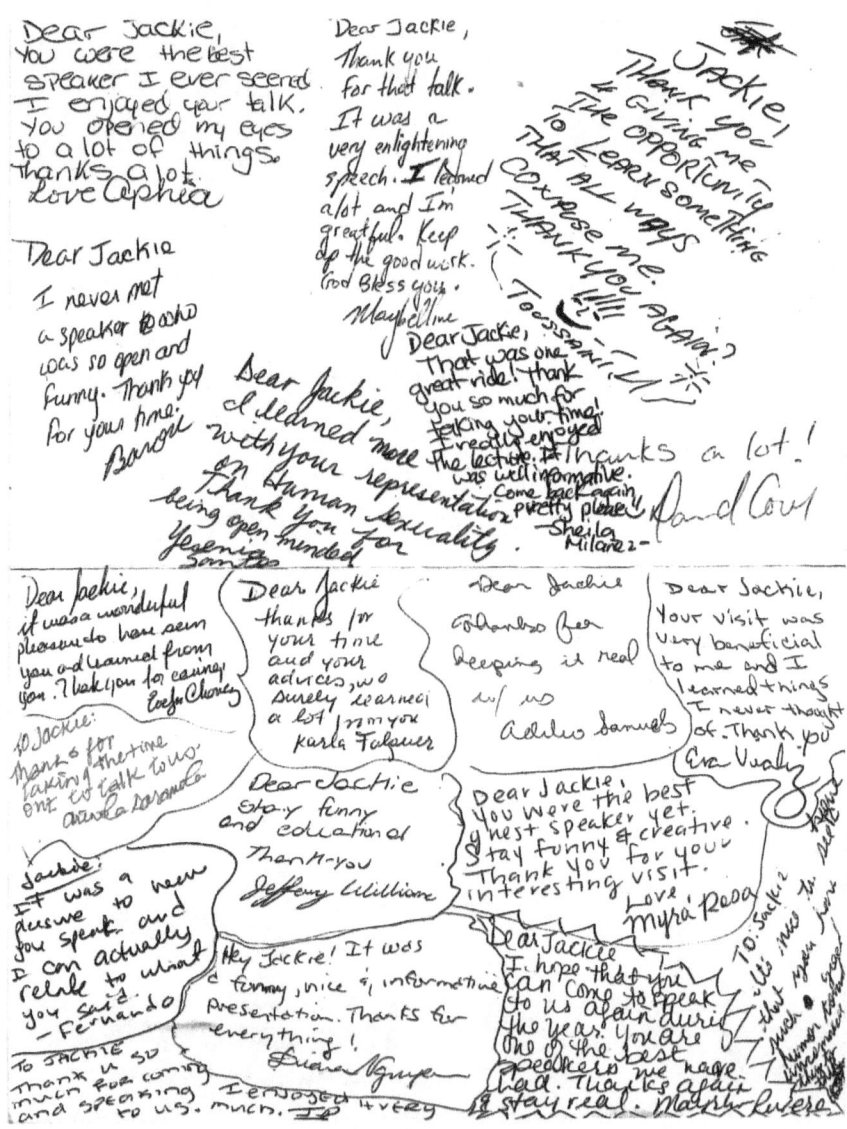

www.ingramcontent.com/pod-product-compliance
Lightning Source LLC
Chambersburg PA
CBHW030531290526
45786CB00004B/1682